DATE DUE

Bobby Discovers Bird Watching

BOBBY DISCOVERS BIRD WATCHING

Text by Marjorie Wackerbarth

Illustrations by Lawrence Spiegel

Publishers
T. S. DENISON & CO., INC.
Minneapolis

T. S. DENISON & COMPANY, INC.

First Printing—March 1963
Second Printing—April 1964
Third Printing—October 1964
Fourth Printing—May 1965
Fifth Printing—January 1966
Sixth Printing—October 1966
Seventh Printing—May 1967
Eighth Printing—July 1967
Ninth Printing—June 1968
Tenth Printing—August 1968
Eleventh Printing—June 1969
Twelfth Printing—October 1970

Standard Book Number: 513-00303-7
Library of Congress Card Number: 62-17849
Printed in the United States of America
by The Brings Press

Minneapolis, Minn. 55431

CONTENTS

BOOKS BY MARJORIE WACKERBARTH
and LILLIAN S. GRAHAM

Bobby Discovers Garden Friends
Successful Parties and How to Give Them
What Is Christmas?
Games for All Ages and How to Use Them
Party Fun for Boys and Girls

To my husband Carl whose help
and kindness have made this
book possible.

HAWKS

Bobby sat on the back porch, his chin cupped in his hands. Just yesterday he arrived for the summer at his grandparents, who lived in a small Iowa town. "This will probably be a dull vacation," he thought. "Grandpa told me that no boys my age live nearby."

Just then Grandpa came into the yard carrying a huge bird. Bobby ran down the porch steps. "What are you doing with that big bird, Grandpa?"

Grandpa put the bird under the cherry tree. Then he tied the leash firmly to the tree. "Bobby, Grandma is right fond of these cherries for pies and tarts. She also likes to have some to can for next winter."

Sparrow
Hawk

Red Shouldered
Hawk

Bobby looked puzzled. "What has that to do with the big bird?"

"This tame hawk belongs to our neighbor. All the smaller birds are afraid of him, so they stay away from this tree and leave the fruit alone."

"I thought hawks were bad birds. Don't they kill chickens?"

"You're partly right. Only two kinds of hawks kill chickens — the chicken hawk and the sharp-shinned hawk. They are both smaller than this fellow here."

Bobby stuffed his hands in his pockets. "What is so good about the other hawks?"

"The red-tailed hawk, the sparrow hawk, and the duck hawk feed mostly on mice, rats, and other small animals that are harmful to farm lands."

Bobby looked up at the sky. "I don't see how a farmer could tell what kind of hawk he was shooting."

Grandpa shook his head. "If he'd take one good look before he shot, he could tell. The red-tailed hawk is easy to recognize. The upper face of the tail is brick red. He has broad wings and a short, rounded tail. When flying his tail is frequently tipped so the upper surface can be seen by ground watchers."

"I'd like to see a hawk like that."

"Maybe we will some day. Look up now, Bobby. That's a sparrow hawk."

Bobby craned his neck. "He's not much bigger than a robin."

"You can tell he's a hawk though by the way he flies. See how he darts through the air, then wheels and turns sharply. Listen! I can hear his cry of 'killy, killy, killy.' "

"Boy, he flies fast!"

"Actually the duck hawk flies faster. He's the fastest flier in North America."

Just then the tame hawk under the tree cried, "Kee you. Kee you."

Bobby whistled in surprise. "Did you hear that, Grandpa? He said, 'See you. See you.' "

Grandpa laughed as he rumpled Bobby's hair. "Did sound like that, didn't it? What he really cried was 'Kee you, kee you.' That's the call of the red-shouldered hawk."

"His shoulders are reddish, aren't they? Does he kill chickens?"

"Oh, no. In the wild he lives on mice and other small animals that are harmful to fields of grain."

Bobby squatted on the ground as he watched the hawk.

"Maybe this fall we can go to Hawk Hill near Duluth, Minnesota. On a good day in September we may see as many as 8,000 hawks all at once."

"Boy, I'd like to see that. Why would we have to go to Duluth?"

"Hawk Hill near Duluth is one of the main flyways for hawks."

"What is a flyway?"

"Hmmm. Guess you'd describe it as a path in the air which thousands of birds follow when they go south in the winter. In this case it is a hawk flyway, because only hawks and falcons follow it."

"Why do they go south? Where do they go? What do they eat?"

"Whoa, Bobby, let's take those questions one at a time. Some go to Mexico and some go to Peru. No one knows exactly why the birds go south unless it is for a more plentiful food supply. Using the same flyways they come north in the spring to raise their families.

"A few weeks before time to leave the birds eat a great amount of food to build up extra fat. Most of this fuel reserve is stored in the abdomen with all organs except the heart adding extra fatty tissue. That way the birds can cover thousands of miles without wasting time in searching unfamiliar territory for food."

"Do all the hawks fly south over Hawk Hill near Duluth?"

"No, Bobby, the hawks have several flyways—down through Michigan, over Hawk Mountain, Pa., and over St. Joseph, Canada. But more hawks fly over the Duluth flyway than any of the others. Starting late in August and continuing to early November bird-watchers estimate a quarter of a million hawks use this one flyway."

"Jeepers, Grandpa. Do other birds use the hawk flyways?"

"No, Bobby. Each kind of bird that migrates has its own flyway. How birds decide where to go we'll never know. Instinct seems to tell each batch of young birds which path to follow even if the older birds aren't with them."

"How come you know so much about birds, Grandpa?"

"I've always watched birds ever since I was a lad your size. You can learn a great deal by just watching them. Then I became interested and have read a lot about them. A scientist who studies birds is called an ornithologist. Birds are most interesting, Bobby. Maybe tomorrow we can go down by the river. There are many birds to watch down there."

"That sounds like fun, Grandpa." Bobby smiled as they trudged back to the house. "Maybe this wouldn't be a dull summer after all."

BOB WHITE—A CLEVER BIRD

Grandpa came around the corner of the house. "What are you doing, Bobby?"

"Nothing," Bobby answered. "I can't think of anything much to do."

"How would you like to take a walk down by the river? We might see something interesting down there."

Bobby couldn't imagine anything of interest along the river, but he didn't want to be impolite. He jumped off the porch railing and went down the dusty road toward the river. The wind in the cypress trees along the stream made a rustling sound.

Suddenly Bobby spotted something beside the path. "Grandpa, look! Here's a dead bird."

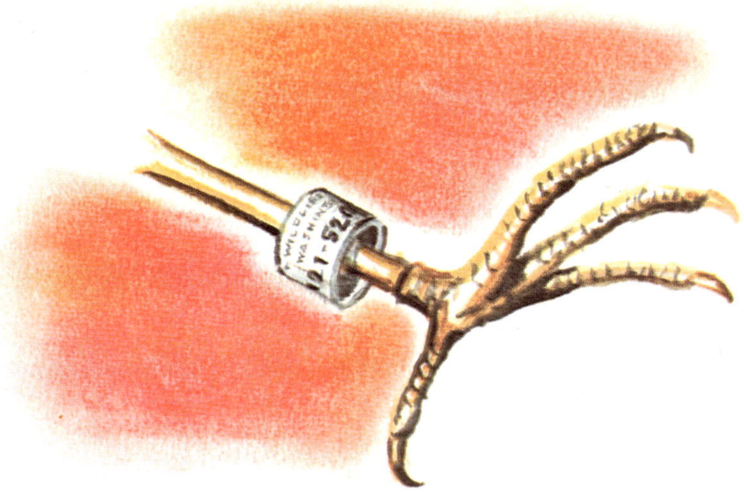

Grandpa squatted beside Bobby. "It's a robin."

Bobby pointed to the narrow metal band on the bird's leg. "Must have been someone's pet bird."

"No, Bobby. This bird was caught by some scientist who is making a study of birds. Look closely. The band has a number on it."

"If the man caught the robin and put the band on his leg, then let him go, what good does that do?"

Grandpa took out his pocket knife to pry off the leg band. "Every time someone finds a banded bird a report is made."

"Why are you taking the band off?"

"We must send this band, with the information about where we found the bird in to the United States Biological Survey in Washington, D.C. That's the place the records are kept. By sending in the band, we'll be helping scientists to study birds."

"It's funny anyone would want to study birds." Bobby couldn't imagine his father taking time for such things.

"Birds are most interesting, Bobby. We know quite a great deal about birds but there is still much to learn."

"What is there to learn about birds?" Bobby was curious.

"A great deal. We know many birds come north in the summer to raise their young. Most of our song birds fly south when cold weather comes."

"Cardinals stay around our yard all winter."

"Oh, sure, some of our song birds stay in the north all year. Besides the cardinals, the bobwhites, Western quail, horned owls, and some of the woodpeckers stay."

“Blue jays and meadow larks and sparrows are always around too.” Bobby was glad he knew something about birds.

“Look, there’s a bird with a broken wing. I’m going to catch it.” With that Bobby ran ahead. The robin-sized bird fluttered along the path, one wing dropping, giving a low plaintive “chink” as it went.

No matter how fast Bobby ran, the brown bird half running, half fluttering, stayed just out of reach. Finally Bobby caught up with the bird. He stooped to grab it. The bird with a sudden whir of its wing and a clear loud “chink,” flew off. Bobby landed on his face.

His grandfather chuckled. “What’s the matter, Bobby? Were you too slow?”

Bobby scrambled to his feet. "That bird wasn't hurt at all. What made it act that way?" Bobby was disgusted.

"That was a bobwhite, Bobby. Some place near where we were, she had a nestful of young ones. She deliberately led us away by acting as if she were hurt."

"I didn't know birds were that smart."

"That's instinct with them, Bobby. Instinct to protect their young. There are several kinds of birds that know that trick, such as grouse and quail. They build their nests so close to the ground, they need some way to call away their enemies."

"I think that's pretty slick." Bobby was impressed in spite of himself.

"Quail, when they roost at night, form a complete circle, like spokes of a wheel, with tails to the center so they can spot danger from all sides. If

alarmed, the birds fly up in the direction they are headed. That way their flight is not concentrated. Hunters have a word for it. They say the birds 'explode.' "

"I'm getting hungry, Bobby. If we went home I think Grandma would have dinner ready."

"Let's go," agreed Bobby, "but we can come again, can't we? This has been fun."

BOBBY FINDS A FEATHER

Grandpa stooped to pick up a feather. "Have any idea what kind of a bird lost that?" Grandpa asked.

Bobby looked at the feather. "It's sort of blue," he said. "Must have been a blue jay. We have blue jays at home." He tossed it on the ground.

"Hold on there, young fellow! You'd better take a good look at that feather. It can tell us lots of things."

Bobby picked up the feather again. He couldn't see anything except that it was blue-gray.

"That's a wing feather, Bobby."

"How can you tell?" Bobby looked again at the feather.

"Because it has a long quill." Grandpa pointed to the center of the feather. "A bird needs stiff feathers on its wings to help it push against the air. That's the way a bird flies."

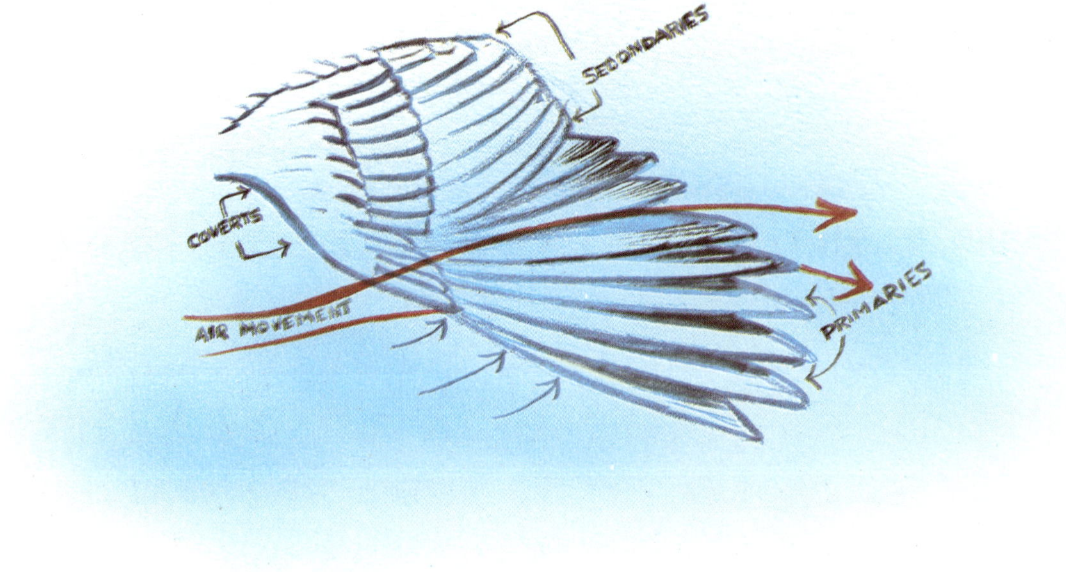

Bobby was interested. "You mean that when a bird flaps its wings, that's what it is doing—pushing against the air."

"Sure, Bobby. You can try it out yourself. The next time you are in a car hold your hand outside the window as you ride along. Tilt it up slightly in the direction you are going and the air will push your hand upward.

"When a bird flies, its wings are tilted in the same way. The front edges of the wings are up and the feather edges behind are down. The air pushing up and the tilt of the wings help to keep the bird in the air."

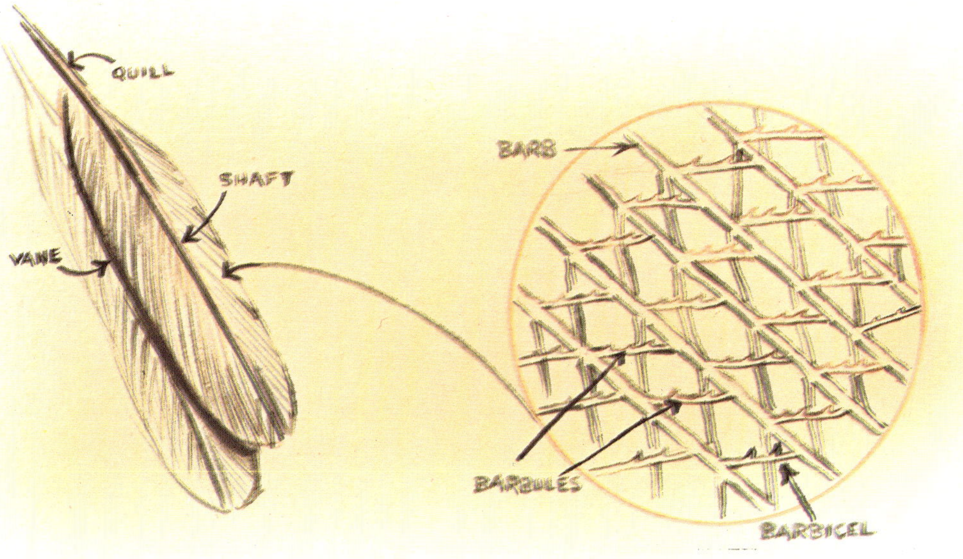

Bobby examined the feather closely. "I'd think the air would slit the feather and it wouldn't hold together."

"Nature has taken care of that too, Bobby. Each bit of feather is interlocked to the next with miniature hooks—too small to see without a microscope."

Bobby threw the feather like an airplane and watched it sail through the air and to the ground. "No wonder a bird can fly so easily covered all over with feathers."

"That's where you are wrong, Bobby. It looks as if a bird is completely covered with feathers, except for the bill and legs. But if it were, a bird would be so hampered that it couldn't fly at all.

"Feathers grow in definite tracts with unfeathered spaces between. There is one big strip of feathers down the middle of the bird's back, another along the undersides of its body, another along the legs. In the large flight feathers of the wings and tail there are bare places."

"Wonder if the blue jay that lost this feather will have trouble flying now." Bobby rubbed his finger along the soft edge of the feather.

"I don't think so," Grandfather chuckled. "Feathers wear out just like clothes. Most birds change feathers once a year—it's called molting. Usually two wing or tail feathers drop out at a time—one on either side of the bird. Then new feathers grow in and another pair drops out. In that way a bird always has enough feathers to fly with."

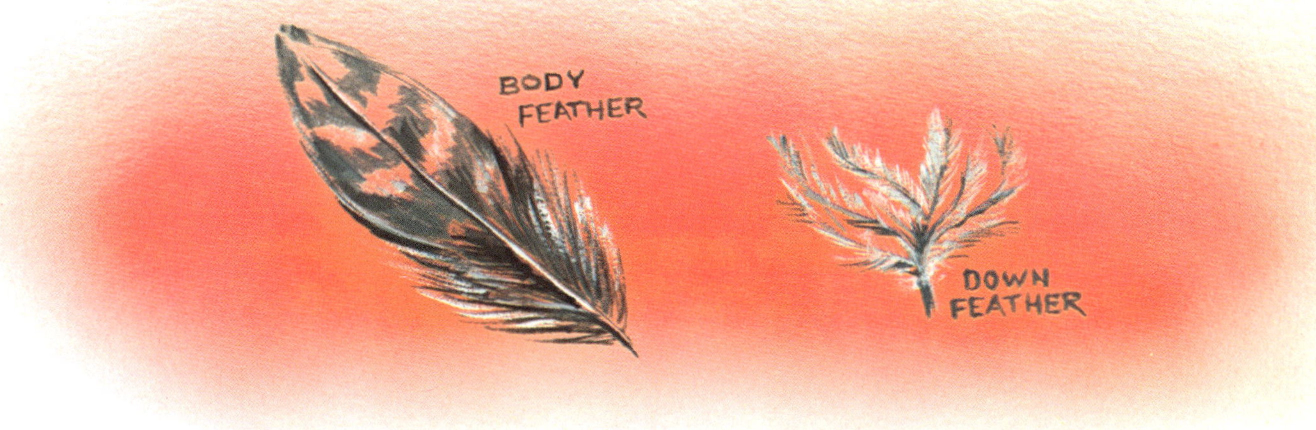

"Say, there ought to be a mate to this feather somewhere around here." Bobby looked down the path.

"Probably there is, Bobby, but the second feather may have floated far away. I wouldn't try to find it now. Some birds like ducks and geese lose so many feathers at a time, they have to hide until they can fly again."

"When are we going to see those birds that nest in the swamp you told me about?" Bobby asked.

"Hold your horses, Bobby. Wait until we get down to the river bank. I think I can show you some things you've never seen before."

LARRY
SPIEGEL

AMONG THE REDWINGS

Bobby and Grandpa soon reached a spot where the river widened, flooding a shallow marshy place.

Bobby pointed to the swamp. "Oh, look, Grandpa, there are birds everywhere."

Grandpa shoved his hat back. "That's right, Bobby. Do you notice anything special about them?"

Bobby looked more closely. "Why, the birds are all alike."

"Sure they are. They're red-winged blackbirds."

Bobby's eyes sparkled as he looked at his grandfather. "I'll bet they get their name from the bright red patch on each wing."

"That's right."

The shrill call of the birds filled the air.

"Must be a hundred or more of the birds."

Grandpa nodded his head. "Probably more than that. Sometimes as many as three hundred will arrive in one flock. Let's move slowly so we won't scare them away. Birds are bothered more with sudden movements than they are with noise."

"These birds are as glossy and as big as robins," Bobby said.

Grandpa stroked his chin. "This whole flock are males."

"How can you tell, Grandpa?"

"The females look more like an overgrown sparrow. Their wings are not as gaily trimmed with bright red patches as the males. Besides the male birds always come north first. Each bird stakes a claim for his future home."

Bobby shoved his hands in his pockets. "Don't tell me that the male birds build the nests all by themselves."

Grandfather laughed. "Course not. The females arrive a couple weeks later. They weave their nests of rushes and sedges and fasten them to the weeds about three feet above the surfaces of the marsh water."

"Isn't that pretty stupid to build their nests so close to the ground?"

Grandpa shook his head. "The red-winged blackbirds are smart. In this marsh they are safe from land enemies and no one can get a boat through that growth of weeds and cattails."

Bobby remembered how hot it can be in the summer on the water in a boat with no shade. "Bet those birds get cooked in hot weather."

Grandpa rubbed Bobby's hair. "The nests are well shaded by the tall weeds and cattails."

"How many eggs are in each nest?" Bobby asked.

"Usually from three to five eggs."

Bobby pulled his slingshot from his pocket. "Bet I could hit one of those birds easily."

Grandpa put his hand on Bobby's shoulder. "Don't ever do that, Bobby. Red-winged blackbirds are too useful to kill."

Bobby looked up in surprise. "What do they do that's so good?"

"They help the farmers by eating grasshoppers and weevils. And they eat weed seeds.

"About two weeks after the males come the females come. Then two weeks later the young males come."

Grandpa sat on a fallen log. "Another unusual thing about these red-wings is they nest closer together than most birds. In other words, they don't stake out such a large area as most birds do."

"What do you mean, Grandpa?"

"People who study birds have discovered that each pair of birds claims a certain amount of ground around their nest. For instance, a pair of robins nests in our back yard. And they won't let other robins nest in that area."

Bobby sat on the log with Grandpa. "How do you know?" Bobby couldn't imagine birds acting like that.

"One day I parked my car in the driveway in my back yard. The male robin kept flying at the shiny hubcap and pecking at it. The female was sitting on a nest of eggs. I took off the hubcap, and the robin paid no more attention to the wheel. Then I put the hubcap back on and the robin started right in diving for the hubcap and pecking at it."

"What made it do that?"

"Well, I finally figured it out. The robin saw his own reflection in the shiny hubcap and thought another robin was trying to invade his territory."

"What did you do?" Bobby was curious.

"As soon as I realized what was bothering the robin, I drove the car farther up the driveway. Evidently, I put it out of the area claimed by the robin because he paid no more attention to the shiny hubcap."

Bobby frowned. "Wonder if all birds stake out claims like that?"

"Scientists tell us that each pair of birds while nesting keeps all other birds of their kind from their area. They have proved that the birds have definite boundary lines. Sometimes these boundaries are no more than a line through the middle of a yard—a boundary no one can see or know about except the birds themselves."

Bobby chuckled. "I had no idea birds were that smart." It was hard for Bobby to realize such things went on in the bird world.

"Birds are mighty interesting, Bobby. The more you watch them and the more you learn about them, the more fascinating they become."

L.C.

THE NUTHATCH

Bobby tugged at his grandfather's sleeve. "Look at that bird going down the tree head first. What kind is that?"

Grandpa turned to see. "That's a nuthatch, Bobby. Any time you see a bird in that position you can almost be sure it's a nuthatch."

"What is he looking for, Grandpa?"

Grandpa stooped to retie a shoelace. "Insects. He will eat nuts and seeds but mostly he lives on insects he finds in the bark of trees."

Bobby frowned. "I don't think I have ever seen a nuthatch before."

"Many people never see nuthatches, Bobby, although they stay all winter long and are plentiful. The white-breasted nuthatch is a small bird with no loud voice or flaming colors. Except for its black cap and some blackish tips on wing and tail feathers, it is blue gray above and clear white underneath."

Bobby watched the nuthatch for a few minutes. "Doesn't he ever feed on the ground?"

"Except for a few of the tamer birds, like sparrows, starlings, or robins, few do. Most birds fly down, grab their food and fly right back to the trees."

Bobby scratched his head. "That's funny. I suppose they are afraid of cats or something."

"Could be. If you watch young birds, you'll see they know how to fly perfectly well before they risk roosting on the ground. After they are good fliers, they will land but then only on a flat space with a clear view all around."

Bobby kicked a stone out of the way as they ambled along. "Don't they have some enemies in the air? Like hawks?"

"Of course they do," Grandpa answered. "But only highly skilled fliers such as pigeons save themselves by outflying their enemies."

Bobby looked up in surprise. "What do other birds do?"

"Different things. For instance, a woodpecker has a funny way of hiding. If a hawk or falcon or some other enemy is overhead, he simply ducks around to the other side of the tree trunk or limb and clings there without moving a feather."

Bobby laughed. "That sounds like a game of hide-and-seek."

"It is. I have seen a woodpecker dodge first one way and then the other, always keeping the branch between him and the enemy."

"Does the woodpecker always win, Grandpa?"

"Almost every time, Bobby."

Bobby pointed excitedly. "Look, Grandpa, high up on the tree is a crow." Bobby was delighted to show Grandpa he knew some birds.

"You know why you can see him so easily, Bobby?"

"Cause he's big and black."

"You're half right, Bobby. His size wouldn't make him conspicuous. It's his solid black color. He's one of the few birds without protective coloring."

"Caw caw!" called the crow as if he knew they were talking about him. "Caw caw," answered a crow from a distance.

Bobby squinted up at the crow. "What do you mean, 'protective coloring'?"

"Well, Bobby, you can spot an all-black crow twice as easily as a many-colored pheasant. A solid over-all color brings out the entire outline of the bird. Speckled colors help to hide it."

Bobby shaded his eyes with his hand. "Almost all birds are sort of speckled, aren't they?"

"That's for their protection. Most birds' enemies approach from the side or above, so their wings, backs and sides are usually colored in a way that imitates bits of dead leaves, grass and twigs."

"You said the crow was one of the few solidly colored birds. Do I know others?"

"Well, the cardinal is almost all red. The all-pink flamingo that lives in the tropics and the all-white egret, a water bird, never are around here."

"I always thought birds had great fun flying all around." Bobby pushed his hands into his pockets. "Sounds like they have their troubles too."

Grandpa laughed. "Sure they have troubles, Bobby, but birds are sociable creatures. Except for nesting time, birds mostly live and fly in flocks. That's another way they protect themselves. If one bird sees an enemy, he gives a warning call. That rouses another bird and he warns others, until often the woods are filled with danger signals."

Bobby brushed a lock of hair off his forehead. "Never thought of it before, but even birds have to be careful, don't they?"

L. SPIEGEL

THE BALD EAGLE

Bobby pointed excitedly to the top of an extremely tall pine on the opposite shore of the river. "That's the highest crow's nest I ever saw."

Grandpa squinted as he looked toward the tree. "That's not a crow's nest. That's an eagle's nest. It's been there a good many years and a pair of eagles use it every year."

Bobby shaded his eyes with his hand. "The nest surely shows up."

"That's because the top of the pine is dead. It can be seen for quite a distance. Each year a pair of bald eagles raise their babies in that nest."

"Are they really bald?"

Grandpa laid his hand on Bobby's shoulder. "No, Bobby, eagles aren't bald. They look bald from a little distance because the feathers on the neck and head are white. The rest of the eagle is dark brown except for the white tail feathers."

SPIEGEL

With its huge wings spread out the bald eagle soared toward the nest. "Boy, I'd like to see that eagle close."

"Even if we could climb that pine, we wouldn't be very welcome. Probably a pair of young ones are in the nest."

"Are they bald too?"

"Only the adults have the white head and tail. The young birds are brown all over. There are a good many kinds of eagles, but the bald eagle is the only one that is a native of America."

Bobby looked at his grandfather. "Is that why the bald eagle was chosen as our national bird?"

Grandpa pulled some change from his pocket. He picked out a quarter and showed it to Bobby. "What do you see on the coin?"

Bobby examined the quarter—first one side, then the other. "Why, Grandpa, there's an eagle on it."

"Sure there is. I haven't a silver dollar with me, but we'll get one the next time we go to the bank. The earlier dollars had the front view of the eagle with wings spread. The later dollars show the side view of the eagle."

Bobby handed the quarter back. "I didn't know the eagle was used so much."

"What's more, Bobby, the eagle is the central figure on the seal of the President of the U. S. In his right foot or talons he holds an olive branch for peace. In his left talons he holds arrows for defense."

"Boy, next time I see a picture of the President's seal, I'm going to take a good look at it."

"Unfortunately, eagles are pretty scarce in some parts of our country."

"Were there ever many eagles?"

"At one time eagles were found in all states. But they are so big and easily seen, many were shot. Besides some people believed wild stories about eagles snatching small children or sheep."

"I don't wonder they shot the eagles then."

"Actually the people were misinformed. Eagles do not steal children or any live animals."

"Funny such stories got started."

"Eagles are so plentiful in Alaska that a bounty of a dollar an eagle was paid for every one shot."

"Why did they do that?"

"Well, the Alaskans had an idea that eagles snatched and killed the baby sea otters that swim alongside the mother sea otter."

"Did the eagles really do that?"

"No, Bobby, scientists after further study found out that the eagles took only the dead otter pups that washed up on the shore. Since 1945 bounties have not been paid on eagles, nor can anyone shoot them. The laws now protect them."

"Do eagles go south for the winter too?"

"Yes, Bobby. The surprising fact is that when traveling they use the same flyways and travel with the hawks. Eagles almost always nest near a stream, lake, or body of water because they mainly live on fish."

"How do they catch them?"

"Eagles really belong to the hawk family. They soar over the water until they spot a fish. Then they swoop down and catch it with their feet."

Bobby looked at his own feet. "I surely couldn't catch anything with my feet. Wonder how the eagle does it."

"Each kind of bird has its particular kind of foot, suited to its needs. The eagle, like its cousin the hawk, has four thick and very powerful toes. Each toe is tipped with long, hooked, sharp nails, because they catch all their food with their feet."

BIRDS' FEET

"Different birds have different feet."

Bobby was puzzled. "All kinds of people have the same kind of feet."

"Sure they do, Bobby. But the kind of foot a bird has depends on how he uses his feet."

"What do you mean?"

"Here's a good example, Bobby." Grandpa stooped down to examine the bird tracks on the muddy shore. "These tracks were probably made by a pheasant."

Bobby bent over—hands at his knees. "How can you tell, Grandpa?"

"These tracks were made by a bird with walking feet like a chicken, grouse or pheasant. The three forward toes are strong and long. The rear one is higher on the leg. That kind of foot is good for scratching, uncovering seeds, bugs or other food. For this rough work toenails are short and stout."

Bobby twisted his foot in the grass. "Next time I get close to a chicken I'm going to look at its feet."

"That's a good idea. And if you see a duck look at its feet. You'll find their three forward toes are joined by a web which turns their feet into paddles. All swimming birds have webbed toes of one sort or another."

"Somehow I never thought about birds' feet."

"A bird's foot can tell you about the bird itself. Humming birds' feet are so little they seem of no use at all. These feet couldn't walk a step. The only thing they ever do is cling to a twig when the hummer wants to rest a bit."

"I know what a humming bird looks like but I've never noticed its feet."

"Most of the common birds we see in our back yard are called 'perching birds,' like the sparrow, jays, blackbird, and chickadee because they can use their feet in many different ways. For instance, blackbirds walk, robins run, sparrows hop, and chickadees climb. All four toes are good-sized and long."

Bobby looked again at his own feet. "Guess the perching birds have the best feet of all."

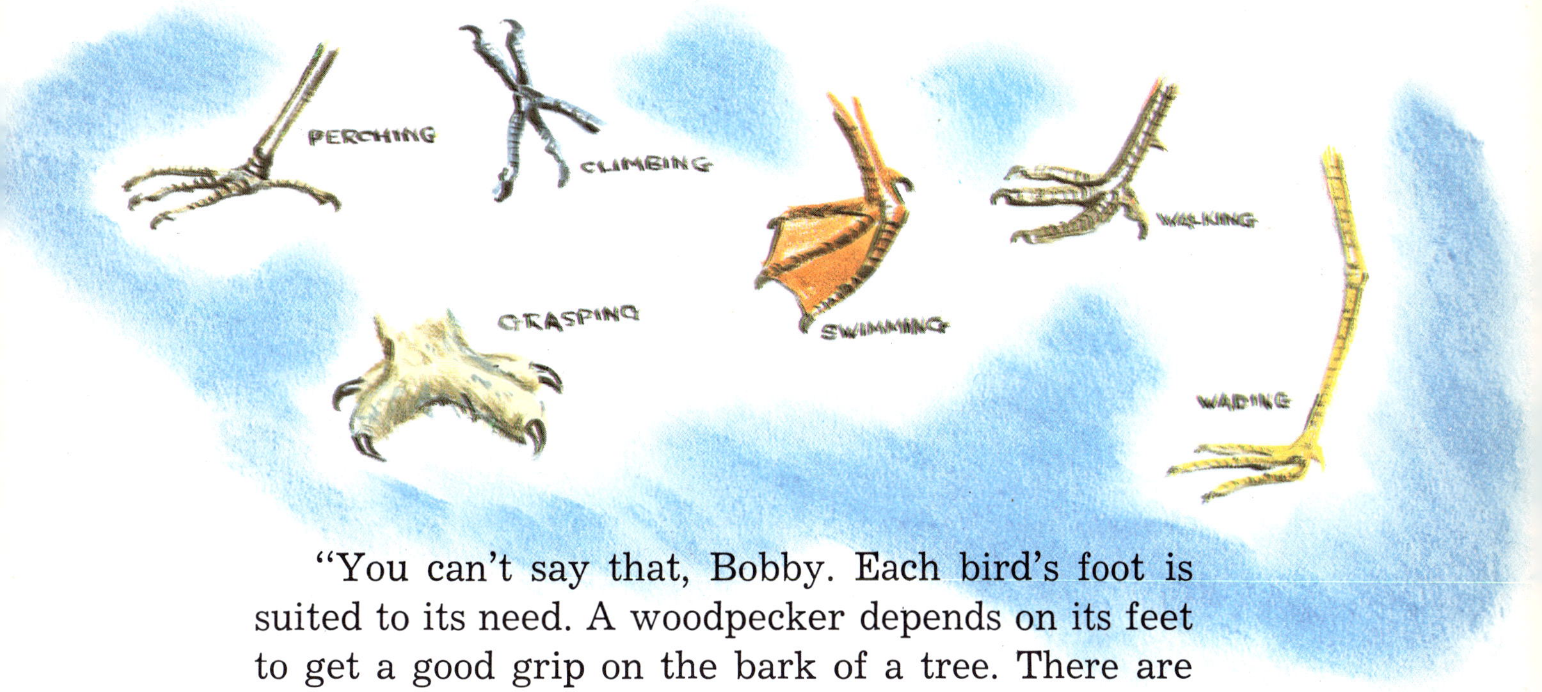

"You can't say that, Bobby. Each bird's foot is suited to its need. A woodpecker depends on its feet to get a good grip on the bark of a tree. There are twenty-eight different kinds of woodpeckers but they all have the same kind of foot—two long-clawed toes in front and two behind."

For a moment Bobby watched a woodpecker chopping away on a nearby tree. "I've often wondered how woodpeckers hang on like they do."

"Look closely at that woodpecker, Bobby. Notice how he uses his tail feathers as support. His tail feathers are long, stiff, and sharp pointed. He pushes his tail feathers into the bark and it makes a first class prop. He uses his tail to help his feet."

"Jeepers, Grandpa, I didn't realize birds' feet could be so interesting. From now on I'm going to look at their feet."

BIRDS HELP COLUMBUS

Grandpa sat on the back porch whittling when Bobby joined him. "What are you making, Grandpa?"

"I'm carving a bird." Carefully Grandpa shaped the bird's bill.

"Wish I could whittle like that."

Grandpa reached into his pocket. "It just happens that I have an extra knife. Run over to the kindling pile and bring a piece of pine about the size you want."

Bobby didn't need a second invitation. He sprinted over to the woodpile and was back with a piece of wood in a few minutes.

Grandpa handed Bobby the knife. "Remember always to cut away from your hand—never towards it. That way if the knife slips it won't hurt you."

Bobby busily smoothed the wood.

"Did you know, Bobby, that birds helped Columbus discover America?"

Bobby stopped his work. "You're fooling me, Grandpa."

"No, I'm not. You have probably read in your story books that after Columbus had been out at sea for sixty-eight days, and out of sight of land for thirty days, his sailors became frightened and wanted to turn back."

"I remember that, Grandpa."

"Actually the sailors demanded that Columbus turn back or they would do it without his orders. In other words they were going to mutiny."

"What did Columbus do?"

"He tried to talk the sailors out of it. He said that they had come so far they would surely find the Indies before long."

"He was looking for another route to the Indies, wasn't he?"

"That's right. Columbus finally coaxed the men to keep going a while longer."

Bobby picked up his wood and whittled some more.

"Just then one of the sailors spotted a whole flock of birds, hundreds of them, flying from the north to the southwest. Columbus then decided that the birds must know the direction to go for land."

"Was Columbus going in the right direction?"

"No, he had been sailing north, so then he ordered the three boats, the Santa Maria, Nina, and Pinta, to change their course and follow the path the hundreds of birds were following toward the southwest."

"What kind of birds were they?"

"Of course, Columbus didn't know. They were different than any birds he had ever seen. Since then ornithologists have discovered that the golden plovers and Eskimo curlews are the only birds with the speed and power to make the overseas flight of 2,500 miles or more from Labrador in the north to the region of the Orinoco River in South America."

"Boy, that's a long way to fly."

Bobby held up his wood. "What do I do now?"

"Whittle just a little at a time until you have the general shape of a bird. It's probably easiest to start the head and back of the bird.

"Columbus and his men changed their course and followed the birds to the southwest for four days at 70 leagues a day."

Bobby stopped whittling for a little. "How far is a league?"

"A league is about three nautical miles—that means he covered about 210 miles a day for four days. Still no land was in sight. The sailors lost faith in the birds. They insisted that Columbus turn back toward home while there was still a chance of making it."

"What did Columbus do then?"

"He still believed the birds were headed for land and pleaded with the sailors to follow the birds for a few more days. If they didn't sight land, he'd turn back."

"The very next day, October 11th, Columbus spotted some sparrows that he knew were land birds."

"I thought our sparrows were brought over from England."

"The English sparrows were, Bobby, but there are many different kinds of sparrows and some of them are native to America."

Bobby resumed his whittling. "What happened then?"

"When Columbus saw the sparrows he knew they couldn't be too far at sea. He shouted to his men in the other boats to watch out for land."

"Did they see land right away?"

"Not until the clouds moved away. Then in the bright moonlight at 2 a.m. they saw land."

"That was the new world Columbus was looking for, wasn't it?"

"Remember, Bobby, that Columbus was seeking a new way to the Indies, but he actually had found a new world—new to people, but for the birds it was a land they had always known."

Bobby picked up his block of wood. "I think I'll try to carve a sparrow like the ones that helped Columbus so much."

"That's a good idea. Maybe I can help you with it a bit."

THE ECHO

"Grandpa! Grandpa! Come here quick." Bobby stood in the backyard all excited. "I have found an echo."

Grandpa came out the door with his field glasses in his hand. "What do you mean, 'an echo'? There are no echoes in this flat country. To get an echo, there have to be hills, rocks or cliffs for the sound to bound back."

"Well, I hear an echo. Come on out to the pump, and I'll show you."

Bobby raced to the pump in the backyard. "This pump squeaks."

Grandpa laughed. "I know it squeaks, Bobby. It's so old and we seldom use it now that we have running water in the house."

"Just listen, Grandpa. After I quit pumping, you can hear the echo of the squeak." Bobby pumped furiously for several minutes. Every time the handle went down, the pump went "squeak, squeak."

Then Bobby stopped pumping. Sure enough from a distance sounded "squeak squeak" exactly like the old pump. "Hear that echo?"

"That's not an echo, Bobby. That's a mockingbird."

"You're fooling, aren't you, Grandpa?"

"No, I am not. When you called about an echo, I suspected a bird. That's why I brought my field glasses. Pump again, Bobby, and we'll see from which direction the sound comes."

Bobby pushed hard on the pump handle. "Squeak, squeak," complained the pump.

From the top of the telephone pole came the answering "squeak, squeak."

"Just what I thought—it's a mockingbird."

Bobby tugged Grandpa's sleeve. "Let me see."

Grandpa handed Bobby the field glasses. "Hold them up to your eyes, then turn that center piece until you can see clearly. Look at the top of the telephone pole. Do you see a bird?"

"It isn't a big bird, Grandpa."

"No, it's about the size of a robin, only slimmer. What else can you see?"

"Its breast is dirty white. Its wings are very dark barred with white, and it has quite a long black tail edged with white. Tell me about him, Grandpa. Can he imitate every sound?"

"I don't think so. His scientific name is Mimus polyglottos, which means many-tongued. Ornithologists have kept track of some of his imitations, and they say he can imitate twenty-eight different bird songs."

"I'll bet he has fun."

"He probably does. He's fond of people and likes to nest where people live rather than in the woods."

"Doesn't he have a song of his own?"

"Sure he has. If you're through watching him, let's go sit on the back steps. Looks like Grandma has put out some lemonade and a plate of cookies for us."

Bobby handed Grandpa his field glasses. "What are we waiting for? That drink looks good."

Between gulps of lemonade, Bobby asked, "Is the mockingbird common?"

Grandpa set his glass down. "Originally he lived only in the south. Southerners like him a great deal. Florida, Tennessee, Arkansas, Mississippi, and Texas all have named him as their state bird."

Bobby ran his tongue over his lips. "How did he get up north then?"

"I don't exactly know. He doesn't go south for the winter. At first we heard that he was in the central states. Then I read about a woman living in Maine who had a mockingbird nesting in her yard. She put out food for it. She found out he liked raisins and peanut butter especially well. At Christmas time she hung a wreath on her front door and he ate all the holly berries."

Bobby chuckled. "Bet she was sore at him."

"She said she didn't mind because he sang so beautifully, especially at night when the moonlight was bright."

"I thought birds sang only in the daytime."

"Usually they do and then mostly in the spring. But not our friend the mockingbird. He sings all season long and especially at night. His song is so much like the European nightingale's song that he is called the nightingale of America."

"You keep saying 'He.' Doesn't the female mockingbird do any singing?" Bobby reached for another cookie.

"Mrs. Mockingbird sings only in the late fall after her family is grown and out of the nest. The mockingbird not only sings but he has a distinctive dance."

"Do the mother and father dance?"

"No, it is only the males that dance. Two birds light on the ground, face each other, heads and tails up. One bird hops two times to the right. The second bird does the same thing. Then they repeat this cake walk to the left. Then they hop forward, beak to beak, then drop back and start over again."

Bobby wiped the back of his hand across his mouth. "Wonder why they do that?"

"It's a sort of ceremonial border dance — two males challenging each other to cross a border line."

Bobby cocked his head listening to the mocking-bird sing. "He sings better than the canary Mom has at home."

"I think so too. Because of his beautiful song years ago people kept mockingbirds in cages, like they do canaries or parakeets now."

"I wouldn't think the mockingbird would like that."

"I heard a funny story about the mockingbird."

Bobby was always eager for a story. "Tell me about it."

"Remember when you went to Florida with your mother and dad and saw Bok's famous singing tower?"

"Sure. A man plays music in the tower with bells."

"That set of bells is called a carillon—the finest in America. Mr. Bok had the idea that it would be nice to have some birds sing in the park too. So he brought some nightingales from Europe and put them in cages throughout the park. He had only five or six of them and they sang beautifully. Mr. Bok was very pleased."

"A few nights later, he brought some friends to hear the nightingales sing when the carillon played. To his amazement the whole park seemed to be filled with nightingales."

"Did someone else bring in some nightingales?"

"No, what happened was that the mockingbirds which are plentiful in Florida were just imitating the nightingales. Other mockingbirds heard them and joined in until you could hear the nightingale song all over the landscape."

Bobby jumped up, wiped his hands on his jeans. "I'm going to make the pump squeak some more and see if the bird will still mimic it."

Grandpa arose too. "Hold on, Bobby. I've a better idea than that. Let's you and me whistle a tune and see if our friend won't sing it too."

"That'll be fun," Bobby agreed. "Let's whistle 'Yankee Doodle.' " By the time they were half way through the song, the bird was whistling with them.

AN OVERNIGHT TRIP— OWLS AND WHIPPOORWILLS

Bobby was just dropping off to sleep when he was startled by "Hoo, Hoo, Hoo, Hoo." Bobby and Grandpa were on an overnight trip in the rugged hills of eastern Iowa.

Bobby reached over and tugged at Grandpa's covering. "Grandpa, wake up. Someone's yelling who, Whoo! at us."

Grandpa chuckled. "We have a hoot owl for a neighbor, Bobby. Get on your shoes. Maybe we can see him with my flashlight."

Grandpa flashed his light here and there. He soon spotted an owl on a nearby branch. His tufted ears erect, the owl turned his head slowly from side to side.

"What big eyes he has."

"It's the white ring of feathers around his eyes that make them appear so big. They show up against his brown body color. Take a good look at him and then we'll go back to sleep."

"Boy, he looks big!"

"He is also known as the great-horned owl. He's our only large owl with ear-tufts. In flight his huge wings stretch out to a span of about four and one-half feet."

"Why haven't I seen him before?"

"Mainly because owls are night birds. They do all hunting and feeding at night."

"How can they see?"

"They see better in the dark than in the daylight. The hoot owl is a lazy bird. He never makes a nest of his own. Instead he takes over a crow's discarded nest or a squirrel's nest. He settles down in the nest until it's big enough for him. By the time the owl is ready to lay its eggs the nest resembles just a bunch of sticks."

"Look how his ears stand up, Grandpa."

GREAT
HORNED
OWL

SCREETCH
OWL

"He just sits there, looking from side to side, as if he's a judge or something."

"Maybe that's why we often hear the expression, 'wise old owl.' He's not really any wiser than most other birds. With his big eyes and large head he just looks that way."

Grandpa flashed his light up and down the tree trunk. "Look, Bobby, at that hole in the tree."

Just before the tree branched was a big cavity. Out of it peered a much smaller owl with little ear tufts.

"Is that a hoot owl's baby?"

"No, remember the hoot owl has his nest high in the tree that's mostly just a bunch of sticks.

"This is a screech owl, the only small owl with ear tufts. Actually it's not much bigger than a robin but with its larger head and puffy feathers it looks much bigger. It always nests in a cavity or hole in the tree."

"Why is it known as a screech owl?"

"Because it occasionally screeches, but mostly it makes a soft musical whinnying note."

"I didn't know there was more than one kind of owl."

"There are at least eight different kinds of owls, Bobby. And maybe more that I don't know about. Let's get back to bed, or we won't get any sleep."

Bobby and Grandpa pulled off their shoes, hung them upside down on sticks, and crawled into their sleeping bags.

Just then Bobby heard "Whippoorwill, Whip-poor-will." "Grandpa, Grandpa! Is that a bird?"

Grandpa raised up on one elbow. Again came the cry "Whip-poor-will." "That's a whippoorwill, Bobby."

"He must get his name from his call."

"He does. He's an odd, big-headed bird, with a short bill, but an enormous mouth. His mouth is fringed with bristles, which makes it a perfect insect net. He swoops back and forth through the evening and night with his big mouth open, gathering his insect prey as he goes."

"Whip-poor-will," the bird called again.

Bobby laughed. "He makes no secret that he's around, does he?"

"I'll say not. One naturalist reported he heard one bird call 'whip-poor-will' 1088 times in one night. Another recorded his song 1,226 times in unbroken repetitions."

"Why don't we see him in the daytime?"

"Because he's a night bird. By day he sits in some sheltered dusky spot on a log or large stone. His brown-black-gray colors blend almost perfectly with his perch."

"I'd certainly like to spot him in the daytime."

"He's pretty hard to find. Unless you lie down and go to sleep I'll think you are a night bird."

Bobby snuggled down into his sleeping bag. "Okay, Grandpa, I'll go right to sleep."

CAMP ROBBER

After a hearty breakfast, Bobby and Grandpa walked to the highest hill so they could look at the mighty Mississippi. Bird songs and calls, some sweet, some raucous, filled the air with sound.

"All the birds in the world must be here this morning." Bobby scrutinized every tree to see as many of the birds as he could.

Grandpa cleared his throat. "Noboby knows how many birds there are in the world. It runs into millions. It is estimated we have 1,400 different kinds of birds in the U. S. alone."

"Wow! I had no idea there were that many birds in our country."

Grandpa looked at his watch. "Guess we better pack our gear and head for home. We have a hundred miles to go."

As Bobby and Grandpa approached camp, Grandpa laid a hand on Bobby's shoulder. "Look at that big bird. That's the first time I have ever seen that bird this far south."

The bird hunted around the camp busily for scraps of food. Presently he flew away with a scrap of bacon. "That's a nervy bird coming right up to our camp for food. Looks like he's a big chick-a-dee."

"He does look like a chick-a-dee, but he's really a Canada jay. He's known by a number of names, though. Some people call him moose bird. That's because he often roams with wild moose. At the approach of hunters he sounds a loud warning."

"I imagine the moose are glad to have that bird for a friend."

"I suppose they are," agreed Grandpa. "Another name for that same bird is 'Camp Robber' and after what we've just seen it's easy to imagine why he has that name."

"I'll say." Bobby chuckled at the idea of a bird being a robber.

"Up north these same birds flock around lumber camps and are known as 'Lumberjacks.' They are not finicky when it comes to food. Refuse heaps and kitchen garbage are carefully worked over for bits to eat."

"Wonder why this bird came this far south."

"There are a dozen varieties of the Canada or gray jay. Some are found as far south as Arizona and New Mexico, Bobby. In this section of the country they are seldom seen outside the dense evergreen forests, and at nesting time they retreat to densely wooded, almost inaccessible swamps of the north."

"Do they build their own nests in the spring?"

"These birds are different that way too. They build their nests in February while the snow is still on the ground and the temperature is far below zero."

"They must build warm nests."

"They are good architects and build very warm nests of twigs, strips of bark, grasses and moss. And most surprising of all, these are all bound together with the silk of spiders."

"Where do they get the spider silk?" If anybody but Grandpa had told that to Bobby, he would have thought they were making it up. But Bobby knew if Grandpa said so, he really meant it.

"Probably from cobwebs they find here and there. The nest is deep, lined with fine grasses and also has a warm inner lining of feathers and hair."

"How many babies do they raise?"

"Usually from four to six. While these birds will eat wild berries they are especially fond of insects and meats."

"Do you suppose the Canada jay is related to the blue jay, Grandpa?"

"Yes, Bobby, it belongs to the same family but it is always a soft gray, instead of blue and has fluffy plumage."

"I still wonder why the bird came this far south."

"Who knows? Maybe he likes this wild wooded area. The Canada jay is not only known by many different names but he also has so many different calls he is hard to recognize. Woodsmen say that a strange noise in the north woods is pretty sure to mean a jay is about."

"Do they chatter like a blue jay?"

"Yes, and they utter loud whistling notes, scold like a red squirrel, and in breeding season they sing like a catbird."

"Pretty good, I'd say."

"They are always on hand to investigate any strange sight or sound in the woods. They are not dull company and woodsmen enjoy them throughout the long winters."

Bobby picked up a round, smooth, flat stone. "Did you ever see such a flat stone?"

"Put it in your pocket, Bobby. When we get home I'll show you how to skip flat stones across the river."

Bobby pocketed the stone. "That'll be fun."

Grandpa laughed. "We'd just better pack our gear in the car and head for home, or we won't get there to skip stones."

A PATRIOTIC TRAY

"It's so much fun watching birds, I'm going to miss it this winter." Bobby and Grandpa both sat on the back steps whittling.

"No reason you can't enjoy the birds this winter, too, if you make a bird-feeding tray."

"A tray would be pretty hard to make, wouldn't it?"

"Depends on the kind you make. The kind we had last winter was very simple, yet we had just as much fun as if we had a fancy one."

Bobby was immediately interested. "Could I make one?"

"Sure you could. You could make it today. When you go home, you'd have it ready to take with you."

"Swell!" Bobby closed his jacknife and put it in his pocket. "Where do we start?"

Grandpa laughed. "You don't waste any time, do you, Bobby? You know that empty apple box in the basement?"

Bobby jumped up. "Should I go get it?"

"Just the wooden box cover, Bobby. While you're getting that, I'll go out to the woodshed and find some thin strips of wood to nail around the edges."

Bobby raced downstairs as fast as he could go. He returned almost immediately with the box cover in his hands. "Is this what we need?"

"That's it, Bobby." Grandpa sorted the wood he had. "Think these thin strips will just do the trick. Bring out some small nails and a hammer from the tool box. I'll get the saw."

Bobby watched as Grandpa measured the thin wooden strips.

"You hold the box cover on the edge, Bobby, and I'll nail the wood around the sides."

Bobby grasped the solid piece of wood with both hands, while Grandpa nailed the strips of wood on first one side, then another.

"What are those for, Grandpa?"

"These edges are just high enough to keep the scraps of food and seeds from rolling off."

"That didn't take very long, did it?" Bobby looked at the piece first one way then another. "It's just like a tray, isn't it? But what do I do with it?"

"Last winter we had one. I nailed it to the outside sill of the kitchen window, and braced it up with two strong pieces of wood. It would be all right to put it on top of a post or stump near the window."

"Would it be best to fasten it to the window sill?"

Grandpa smoothed a rough edge with his knife. "Any place will do, but it's handy to have it near enough to the window so that food can be put out through the raised window. Last year we called ours a 'patriotic tray.' "

"A patriotic tray!" exclaimed Bobby. "Did you paint it red, white, and blue?"

Grandpa laughed. "No, Bobby, our colors were live."

Bobby frowned in puzzlement.

"That's not a hard riddle, Bobby. The cardinals that came to feed were red and the jays blue."

"Yes, but where did you get the white?" Bobby asked. "Oh, I know, the snow was white."

"Of course, snow is white, but this time we had something more exciting. You'd guess a long time before you'd think of the right answer. It was an albino sparrow."

Bobby whistled, "An albino sparrow! You mean a pure white sparrow?"

"Yes, naturalists have recorded among others albino ring-necked pheasant, meadow lark, robin, crow, blackbird, mourning dove, quail and goldfinch."

"I'd surely like to see an all-white sparrow," Bobby said as he examined the newly-made tray. "Aren't covered feeders better than just a tray?"

"Covered feeders are fine, but birds go to an open one just as readily," Grandpa explained. "Nature has given each little bird a heart that beats so rapidly his little body is a regular furnace. For instance, a chick-a-dee's heart beats 600 to 1000 times a minute."

"What can I feed the birds?" Bobby said, puzzled.

"Bread is always a stable food for birds, but the regular food supply should consist of seeds of almost any kind—sunflower seeds, rape seeds, millet, canary bird mixture and wheat screenings."

"Do all birds eat the same kind of food?" Bobby wrote down on an old envelope the food Grandpa mentioned.

"Nutmeats and doughnuts are liked especially by woodpeckers, chick-a-dees, nuthatches and creepers."

"Boys like that kind of food too."

Grandpa laughed. "I know they do, but if you want to feed the birds you'll have to share with them."

"That won't be too bad." Bobby continued to make his list.

"We always fasten a piece of suet to a tree. Birds love suet."

"How do you keep jays from carrying it off?"

"Grandma has an old-fashioned wire soap holder that she fills with suet and hangs on the tree. But any kind of chicken wire can be used to hold the suet and still the birds can peck at it. When the weather isn't too cold, you can put out a dish of water for them."

"Must be tough for birds when the ground is all covered with snow," Bobby said thoughtfully.

"It is. That's why we like to feed them. We always put out a little sand and gravel, and we mix a little salt with it."

"Is that to keep it from freezing?"

"No, salt is good for birds, especially the sparrows, but it must be mixed with fine earth."

Bobby turned to the tray, examining it from all sides. "Boy, it's going to be fun to feed the birds this winter."

"It is fun. You'll be surprised, too, at how many transient birds stop to feed on their way to their winter homes. Don't be disappointed if you don't get many birds at first. Sometimes it takes a little while for them to spot the feeder, but they are sure to find it in time."

"Thanks a lot, Grandpa. I know Dad will help me set it up when I get home."

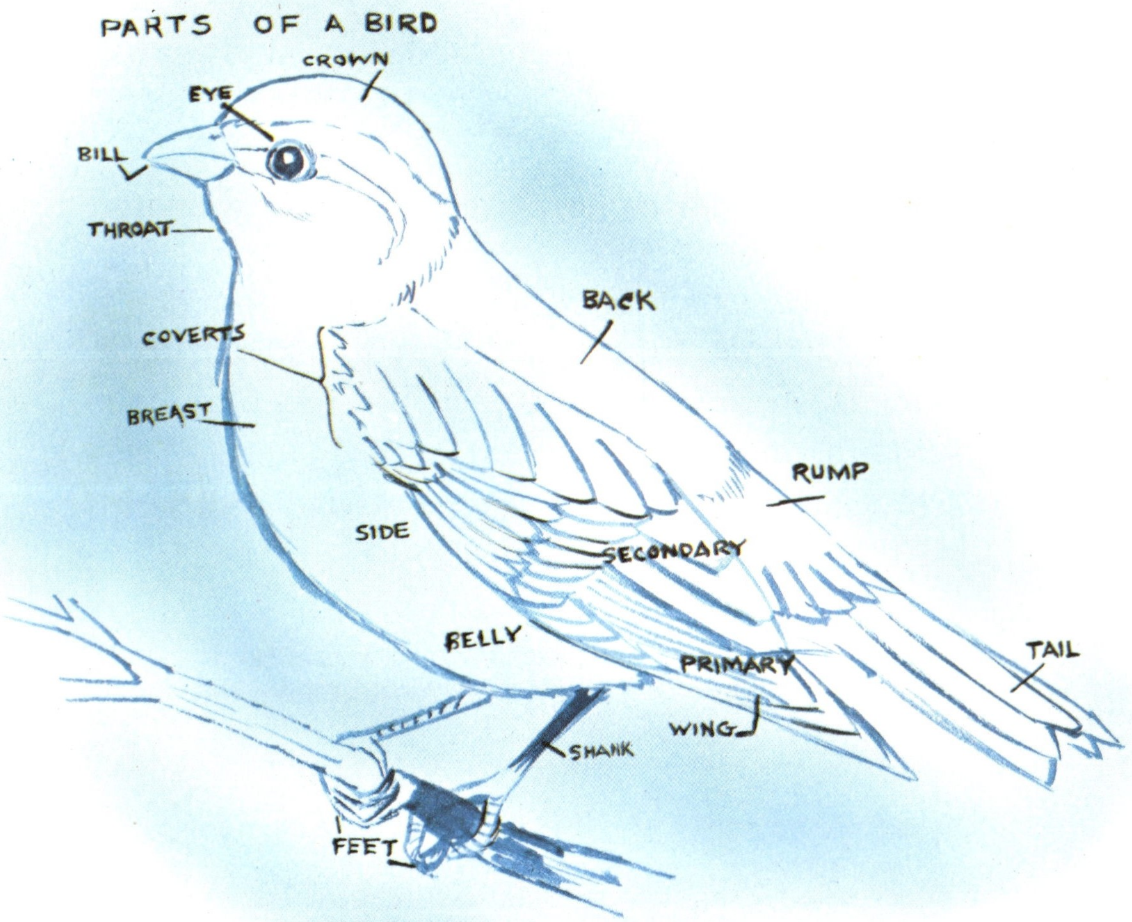
PARTS OF A BIRD
CROWN
EYE
BILL
THROAT
BACK
COVERTS
BREAST
RUMP
SIDE
SECONDARY
BELLY
PRIMARY
TAIL
WING
SHANK
FEET